# her
# path
# forward

## 21 stories of transformation and inspiration

a modernwell anthology
edited by julie burton and chris olsen

HER PATH FORWARD: 21 STORIES OF TRANSFORMATION
AND INSPIRATION (V2)
© Copyright 2021 Julie Burton and Chris Olsen

ISBN: 979-8-9850242-1-0
Library of Congress Control Number: Pending
Printed in the United States of America
First Printing: 2021

Published by Publish Her, LLC
2909 South Wayzata Boulevard
Minneapolis, MN 55405
www.publishherpress.com

PUBLISH **HER**™

"We delight in the beauty of the butterfly, but rarely admit

the changes it has gone through to achieve that beauty."

–Maya Angelou

# introduction

From Julie Burton and Chris Olsen,

Editors of "Her Path Forward"

P eople cross paths at different times for different reasons. When our paths converged at ModernWell in 2018, neither of us knew exactly why we were meant to meet. But for the next three years, we continued to learn more about each other and the ways in which our lives, interests and passions intersect. From sharing Saint Paul roots, to pursuing careers in media and marketing, to enduring major changes in our lives that resulted in creating our respective businesses, a powerful connection emerged.

Beyond our common birthplaces and professions, we soon learned the most exciting part of our connection is an unrelenting dedication to elevating the words, stories and writing of women. Partnering on a project that would bring women's stories to life would be a natural next step for us. Since we'd both experienced life-altering events that shaped who we would become, we decided to utilize the concept of transformation as the theme for our book of essays.

Our communities of writers and storytellers came forward and sent so many powerful and unique essays. The stories illuminated just how intimate change can be—that we all transform in our own way, at our own pace, and on our own path. And regardless of how or when or why one transforms, the essays illustrated just how much change is an essential part of growth and life. And, as we discovered, when a woman emerges anew and transformed, there is often magic to be found in the space where her path intersects with another's.

"Her Path Forward" is a collection of 21 essays that elevate the various perspectives of women navigating change and the path forward. We are so grateful to the authors of these essays for being courageous and vulnerable and sharing their words and writing. It is our honor to bring them to the world.

*About Julie and Chris:*

*Julie Burton is an author, co-host of Her Next Chapter podcast, and founder of ModernWell, the first female-centered co-working and collaborative space in Minneapolis, Minnesota, dedicated to empowering women through connection, wellness and creative freedom. Julie is also a mom of four and believes that an important piece of living a purposeful and fulfilled life is allowing yourself the space and freedom to evolve and transform.*

*Chris Olsen is dedicated to amplifying women's voices through her social enterprise, My Founder Story, a storytelling and publishing platform. A radio veteran turned communications consultant, educator and author, Chris is passionate about empowering female business founders in confidently communicating their purpose and impact, setting them up for entrepreneurial success. Since 2018, My Founder Story has donated more than $220,000 in grants and services to women.*

# our path forward

By Julie Burton

It was different this time. But the same. It was grief laced with fear and set on fire by the invisible churning, rearranging hormones that raged inside of me. Another perfect storm. Another collapsing of my being, my spirit. The spinning of anxiety and depression came in the form of ravaging guilt, shame, self-blame and regret. For not knowing the answers. For being paralyzed with fear about making a wrong decision. About my four children. About my life. I should just know. How could I *not know* what I was doing, where I was going or how the hell I was going to get there?

It didn't help that there was no there. I could no longer see it. I don't remember if I ever could. There had always been something strong pulling me in a direction that I assumed to be the right path forward. But no more. Midlife would break the needle of my internal compass. I was no longer young, but not completely old. I would have no more babies. My kids would leave the nest. My body would not cycle the way it had for the past 3 ½ decades, guiding me through time and space. Now I was tossing and turning during sleepless nights as heat pulsed through my body and anxious, futile thoughts raced through my brain, leaving me in a pool of sweat and tears.

The only thing left was fight or flight. But I was too tired for both. I felt the fragility of my mental state. The creeping close to the edge of rationality and sanity as panic signals fired from within. *Run and hide, take cover, you are not safe. You. Are. Not. Equipped. To handle your life. Did you get that? Let me tell you again.* Over and over.

Brave. That was what Brené Brown told me to be. "Do the work" was written (by me) on a Post-it note and placed (by me) at eye level on the wall above my writing desk stood, along with other notes and cards of encouragement.

I had done the work on the therapy couch, in my marriage, with my kids, in my writing. My book was headed to the publisher. The words would be imprinted on the pages for all to read and to judge. My secrets. My story. My self-care advice. Advice I was struggling to follow.

On the outside, I was a woman of privilege living a comfortable life raising four privileged children, while working part-time and playing the support role to her husband's budding career.

Lucky her. Lucky me.

Except for the strangling feeling that this was not supposed to be my life, that I was desperately missing something, that I had given up too many parts of myself and didn't really like what was left. It gnawed at me day and night.

I could fill my days. I could helicopter over my children, volunteer for worthwhile causes and organizations, write articles about parenting, co-run a writing studio, inspire my spinning or yoga students in the fitness classes I taught. I could spend time with loving family and friends.

Until I couldn't. Until my body began shutting down its normal functioning and the waves of menopause tossed me into uncharted, unpredictable, rapidly changing water, twisting me upside down and inside out, leaving me rudderless, confused, scared and alone.

And there was Mary Oliver: "What is it you plan to do with your one wild and precious life?"

*I don't know, Mary. I really don't know.*

I had to lie down. For a while. Weeks. Months. Friends and family had to feed me and take me for walks. I was not okay. Most people didn't know. But those who did worried. I worried. And I prayed.

*Mary, I need things to be different. I need things to be different in my life, my marriage, with my kids, with my relationships. With myself. I need to use my privilege to make a difference in the world. I need to create something that matters. That brings people together. That solves for loneliness. That challenges the patriarchal systems and celebrates the magic in all of us. That gives people permission to expand, explore, create and grow. I desperately need to be in this kind of environment. Surrounded by people who are curious. And motivated. And creative. And innovative. And different from me and each other. Is it a space? Is it a community? What is it? Where is it?*

There was Brené again: "Owning our story can be hard but not nearly as difficult as spending our lives running from it. Embracing our vulnerabilities is risky, but not nearly as dangerous as giving up on love and belonging and joy ... Only when we are brave enough to explore the darkness will we discover the infinite power of our light."

I explored the dark. Not because I wanted to, but because my chemistry, genetics, wiring and hormones took me there.

But the light would be just so Brené—love, belonging and joy. So I would lift my head from my pillow, practice what I preach, set my boundaries, own my worth, create this space. My life depended on it. And I bet that someone else's did too.

*Could it be true, Ray Kinsella/Kevin Costner? If I build it, will they come?*

Thank you for coming.

You are the path forward. You are the inspired community built from pain turned to hope. You've created businesses and books and blogs and podcasts and friendships and healing. You've welcomed world-renowned authors and speakers and thought leaders. You've stood up to sexism, racism and antisemitism. You are women in charge and free to bravely share your stories and pave your own path forward. Maybe at the water cooler, maybe through your work, maybe right here on the following pages.

Transformation is often not pretty. Glennon Doyle would call it "brutiful." It is about letting go of what you should be and listening to the tiny (or blaring) voices inside your head and heart that tell you, *this ain't it—look over there*. Not necessarily the there that is the shiny new pair of shoes or another bottle of wine. But the there that is inside you, the gifts that are yours alone, waiting to be discovered, embraced and shared with the world.

ModernWell is the culmination of all that I was, all that I am, and all that I aspire to be. It is the first female-centered coworking and creative space in Minnesota, where growth and possibilities are endless. ModernWell is my path forward. It is your path forward. It is *our* path forward.

*About the author: Julie Burton is an author, co-host of Her Next Chapter podcast, and founder of ModernWell, the first female-centered co-working and collaborative space in Minneapolis, Minnesota, dedicated to empowering women through connection, wellness and creative freedom. Julie is also a mom of four and believes that an important piece of living a purposeful and fulfilled life is allowing yourself the space and freedom to evolve and transform. www.modernwell.com*

# the only path is forward

By Chris Olsen

T*eratoma. Teratoma. Teratoma.* Like a megaphone-toting member of a bizarre medical condition cheer squad, I repeat the word aloud to myself as I drive home from the clinic. I should've asked my OB-GYN to write it down. Minutes earlier, an ultrasound confirmed a mass on my right ovary, which she'd first felt during an exam. The sonogram revealed it's the size of a Snickers bar. It appears to be a mature teratoma, she said. A kind of mixed matter tumor that is almost always benign.

Benign. That word I know. It's the word my brain is clinging to like a bit of stray yarn stuck to Velcro. Teratoma is more difficult to remember. So I am chanting it like a fight song for the entire drive home. Minutes later, I am sitting in front of my laptop at my dining room table looking at the definition on WebMD:

*Teratomas are rare tumors that may hold different types of tissue such as bone, teeth, muscle and hair. They're mostly found in the ovaries, testicles and tailbone, but also sometimes grow in the nervous system and abdomen.*

In an instant, it comes to me. I've heard about teratomas on an episode of "Grey's Anatomy." Did that patient have cancer? No, I don't think so. This random TV reference gives me hope. Plus, I am too young to be diagnosed with ovarian cancer. It most frequently develops in women 55 to 64 years old, well after childbearing years. I know this because a decade ago my mom was diagnosed with ovarian cancer at age 55. She had no symptoms until it had already ravaged her body. When the surgeon opened her up, he removed the tumors he could and stitched her back together again. Dozens of tentacles still intact, slowly squeezing the life from her. She endured a year of chemo and radiation. In the final months, I put my career on hold to be her full-time caregiver—I became the mother and she became the child.

I'm focusing on my career now and haven't had children of my own yet. My tumor announced its presence a month ago. Then and now, whenever I stand up, a burst of colorless, odorless fluid gushes from my vagina. At first I thought it was my period. But no blood. Then I thought it was a bladder infection. When it first happened, I'd been camped out next to my dad's hospital bed for days, consuming only pretzels and Diet Coke from the vending machine. Dad had just been diagnosed with liver cancer and was expected to die within a week. I couldn't leave him. I assumed the shock, sadness and stress of losing my last living parent was taking its toll and that my body was protesting. Maybe it was. Maybe it is.

As I soak in the bathtub the night before my appointment with the surgeon, I slide three fingers inside myself as far as I can. I shift to the side and for a brief moment, I can feel it pressing against the outside of my uterus—the tumor with bone, teeth and hair. I think about the "Grey's Anatomy" episode. A man walked into Grey Sloan Memorial Hospital with a protruding belly. He was convinced he was having a baby. Turns out it was a teratoma. I wonder if I would've assumed my teratoma was a baby had it grown to basketball size.

In the surgeon's office the next day, I think we'll talk about removing the teratoma. It'll happen after I wrap up a big work project and prep my assistant for what I assume will be my brief absence. I'm certain the surgeon will say the plan is to have the lab biopsy the mass after he extracts it to confirm it's not cancer. I wait for him to reiterate what my OB-GYN said, that mature teratomas are typically benign. Instead, after a brief exam and my account of the clear gushing fluid, he cavalierly says, "We'll get you on the schedule for surgery this Friday. You'll start chemotherapy six weeks after that."

*What the hell are you talking about?* I think. I resist the urge to say it aloud. Instead, I ask why a benign tumor with bone, teeth and hair would require chemo. He confidently tells me it's *not* a teratoma, and I want to know how he can be so sure. He says the clear fluid is a rare symptom of early onset ovarian cancer that something like less than one percent of women experience.

"The good news is we found it now and not a year from now," he says.

Maybe I should feel fortunate. But I don't. Like the man on "Grey's Anatomy," I will never give birth to a baby.

As I'm leaving the clinic, my big brother calls to grumble about having to manage Dad's estate. I tell him I don't care; I've got my own problems to deal with.

Now my phone is ringing and it's my favorite aunt, my fairy godmother. "I don't know what to do," I tell her.

"There's only one thing to do," she says. "Move forward."

She makes it clear that I must keep going full steam ahead. She takes me to the hospital for surgery and vigilantly waits in the lobby while my tumor and life-making organs are removed. She takes me to chemotherapy appointments and crochets soft beanies for my bald head while I sleep through the eight-hour infusions. And in the middle of the night, when I'm sure the drugs meant to save me are actually killing me, she brings me a heating pad to soothe my throbbing kidneys, sits beside me in the dark and assures me tomorrow will be better.

I'm not entirely certain forward is the direction I would've chosen if left to my own devices. But now, 12 years later and cancer-free, I'm grateful for my godmother's nudge—or perhaps shove—onto the conveyor belt. The lessons of my journey continue to reveal themselves: There are not always endless options as we navigate life's path. When facing a fork in the road, we don't always have an opportunity to carefully consider the pros and cons and make an informed decision on which way to go. There will be unexpected storms that roll in and rage hard and steady for days or weeks or months or even years. They may wash out the road completely, making returning to our previous path an impossibility. During those times, there is only one way to go. There is only one path. And it is forward.

*Chris Olsen is dedicated to amplifying women's voices through her social enterprise, My Founder Story, a storytelling and publishing platform. A radio veteran turned communications consultant, educator and author, Chris is passionate about empowering female business founders in confidently communicating their purpose and impact, setting them up for entrepreneurial success. Since 2018, My Founder Story has donated more than $220,000 in grants and services to women. www.myfounderstory.com*

# you'll know when you need to leave

By Sister

I came home from work and a board meeting, and he was passed out with an almost empty bottle tucked in beside him in his black leather chair, next to a dirty fish tank he failed to clean and promised to fill with fish again but never did. I dropped my bags and ran up the stairs. To the left, down the hall past the wallpapered bathroom with ancient fixtures, my 4-year-old daughter was sleeping peacefully in the lower bunk of her bunk bed in her pink bedroom.

Then I ran to her little brother's room with Winnie the Pooh on the wall. His crib was empty. My little boy was just 6 months old. He was perfecting his crawl. His bedroom was next to ours. And that's where I found him. In our room. On our bed, three or four feet off the ground, with blankets and pillows surrounding him. The thoughts collided in my head: *What if he had woken up and crawled off the bed crying? What if he had cracked his head open in the fall? Who would have heard him? Would his sister have run to our bedroom to find his body on the floor? Would she have known to shake her dad awake, to scream that something was wrong?*

Images flashed in my mind of what could have been. My heart racing in fear, I scooped him up from our bed, snuggled his little boy smell, his plump face and warm body, gently put him into his crib and closed his door. Then I packed our bags. *I can do this*, I told myself that night, as I stuffed a handful of my children's clothes and little boy diapers into a small duffle.

I had packed that same bag before. Previous times when I took my kids away from my husband. We slept at his sister's, my sister's, at my best friend's house. We left the time we heard a loud thump upstairs and he was drunk and high on pills and my daughter asked, "What was that, Mommy?" We left the time I found a knife sticking straight up out of a cutting board in the kitchen. We left the time our fridge, usually carefully covered top to bottom in magnetic photos of the people we love, was blank, photos and magnets scattered across the floor. We left just months before, the time he angrily wrenched my cell phone out of my hands so I could not call for help. I had to hide with the children at a neighbor's house, sobbing while her husband drove over to demand my phone back. This time was different. I had been here before. But this time, I was not turning back or giving in.

I whispered under my breath the words I had been told by women who had been where I was before: *You'll know when you know. You'll know when you need to leave.* Women in my small Facebook group, with young children and drunk husbands. We typed long-winded stories to each other late into the night, tears hitting keyboards. I told them how each time he went to rehab my life was calmer. But then he would come home and I would ease myself into the dark corners of his needs, tiptoeing over the shattered pieces of myself so I could try to take care of him. To—impossibly—fix him. *You'll know when you know.* This time I knew.

"You have three days to leave," I told him to his sluggish face and angry eyes. "Pack what you want." I spoke with a strength that came from somewhere deep, somewhere I had forgotten was there.

We escaped to my sister's house for three days. When we came back, he was gone. The kids went to day care and I went to work. This time, with a lighter load than usual, having cracked open my heart to my bosses and handed over projects and travel I could no longer manage into their open arms. And each night after the kids went to sleep, I cried and taped up boxes and cleaned closets and threw away bottles and broken dreams. And then I hired handymen and junk guys and stagers to make the house a home again. But not for us this time. This time, I put the house on the market and left.

We shrunk our life, or so it seemed, moving into a furnished one-bedroom apartment for a month. My world never felt more open. The worst thing that happened that month was my daughter barfing up berries in the king bed we shared. Normalcy was refreshing. Then we packed up again and moved to my little sister's home. My heart was flooded with warmth. The apartment had pared down my life to the essentials: food, a bed, family. Living with my sister and her family started filling me up again, repairing the gaping hole he had carved out of my heart over six years of marriage.

While my sister and my children played together, we cooked

and cleaned and laughed. We listened to music and danced. We pulled our kids in sleds on the lake behind their home and drank hot cocoa in ice houses. We built snowmen and brick towers, and piece by piece I put myself back together. Now I understood—this is what family was supposed to feel like. Love, safety, joy and chaos, all wrapped up together.

I started a Facebook group for local moms raising children on their own, and I learned again—over potluck lunches and play dates—that I was not alone. While my daughter slept beside me, I read books on life after divorce. And then, tiptoeing at first into its sparkling waters, I dove into that life.

*Editors' note: This essay is published anonymously at the author's request.*

# quinceañera

By Astrid Lorena Ochoa Campo

As if sent by Cupid, I landed in the United States on Valentine's Day in 2006. Fifteen years later, the global pandemic did not allow me to celebrate the milestone as I wished. Nevertheless, I had my annual celebratory Wendy's burger in the comfort of my apartment. What do burgers have to do with Cupid? They mix rather well in my story: A burger was my first meal when I arrived at a university campus in Long Island, New York, where my au pair training was taking place. I was one day late to my training. I was supposed to travel on Feb. 13, but the airline asked for volunteers to fly the next day. The reward was one more night in Bogota, Colombia, plus a travel voucher. I did not think twice about it and volunteered.

That extra night, my mom and I had a great time in the hotel and rested adequately. Still carried away by the excitement of traveling abroad for the first time, I did not anticipate the crushing feeling of separation once I went through security and realized I could not hug my mother anymore that day. Even now, when people ask me how I could leave my family behind, I tell them I wasn't thinking. This is partly true. I spent more than a year preparing for the trip, not knowing whether it would happen. But I was not even remotely aware of all that living in a foreign country would entail. No amount of reading and talking can prepare you for it. As we say in Barranquilla about our carnival, *quien lo vive es quien lo goza*. That is, *you have to live through it to enjoy it*.

Fifteen years later, I am a professor, still living in the U.S., now in a part of the country I only knew about through "That '70s Show." I arrived as a young adult, right after my college graduation. I was determined to improve my English skills and hoped to recover from an English class trauma, which involved a professor promising me a cookie if I could pronounce *museum* correctly. I am happy to announce that after all these years I can finally pronounce that word. But I can't differentiate between keys and kiss when I speak. *Pasito a pasito*, as Luis Fonsi would say. *Step by step*. As such, I have been growing even when I think I have not.

If this was my U.S. quinceañera, my slideshow would include pictures of many of my first-time experiences in this country: flying abroad, driving (even in the snow!), bowling, playing softball, hiking, rock climbing, fishing, whitewater rafting, among others. Maybe the scariest of them all—living by myself at the age of 29. I had never done it before because I lived with my parents until I was 24 and then with host families and roommates. I could not say it wasn't exciting, but at times I felt like a character in "One Hundred Years of Solitude." Lonely. Thankfully, the love of God, family and friends helped me through the transition.

My journey from nanny to professor is replete with beautiful memories, as well as less pleasant ones. While I did not plan to become an academic, I was drawn to the teaching profession from an early age. My elementary school teacher thought I could be a good maestra in the future. I got a bachelor's degree in education, came to the United States to study English and enrolled in a master's program and later in a doctorate program. As a result, I have been a teacher for 20 years. I hope to teach for many more years, if my health allows it. By now I have come to understand the toll that getting educated as a woman of color and educating others can take on our physical and mental health. I discovered this during grad school when my body started to protest. The stress I was under as an international student negatively affected my hormonal and immune systems. During my graduate studies, a dear friend recommended counseling and I started going for the first time in my life at age 26. Once I got over my shame of needing support, I learned to ask for it whenever I needed it.

It's funny how life works. In eighth grade, I was playing with some friends, and we each drew a map of our lives. I have no idea why, but my map had me living in the United States, working for NASA and writing a book. I hadn't thought about it again until I found myself living here, not working for NASA, writing my dissertation and thinking about how difficult it was to write it during a pandemic. Instead of writing, I wanted to create memes and maybe become a Facebook comedian—anything to distract me from the hard work of thinking and writing.

I could not have done it without all the support I had from friends and family, for which I am beyond grateful. Finishing the dissertation  project brought me here, from the East Coast to the Midwest. Yet another transition that allowed me to get out of my comfort zone to grow spiritually, professionally and personally. Will I ever work for NASA? Perhaps. I am not sure what kind of job I would do there, given that my training is in literature and cultural studies. But one never knows. For now, I am not volunteering to go to Mars. I need to start writing my book.

*About the author: Astrid Lorena Ochoa Campo is from Barranquilla, Colombia. She is an assistant professor at the University of Wisconsin La Crosse, where she teaches Spanish (language, literature and cultures) and World Language Education. She enjoys spending time with friends and loved ones, reading, traveling and dancing.*

# not done with my changes

By Katie Noah Gibson

*I have walked through many lives,*

*some of them my own,*

*and I am not who I was,*

*though some principle of being*

*abides, from which I struggle*

*not to stray.*

*–Stanley Kunitz, "The Layers"*

I thought I had invented myself by the time I turned 35. A stable, mostly satisfying career (and a good use of my English degrees) working in higher ed communications; a longtime marriage to my college sweetheart; a third-floor apartment we loved, near the running trail I frequented, filled with bookshelves and flooded with light.

We had moved from our West Texas college town after a few years of marriage and grad school, confident we could take on a new city. Proud of ourselves for plunging into the adventure, we had weathered Boston's snowy winters and learned to navigate its illogically twisting streets. We had each hopped around to a few different jobs, but with my new position at a prestigious music college, and my husband's deep love for his work as a therapist, I thought we had finally found our footing.

I wanted to throw my own birthday party, though I worried it would seem egotistical, calling too much attention to myself. But after eight years in Boston, we'd built up a handful of steady friendships and our circles were constantly expanding. We sent out an email to a few dozen people from different areas of our lives: our tiny church, my former workplace at Harvard, the a cappella group my husband used to sing in. I made sure to invite Gamal, the man I had met at a coffee shop two years before, when he was slinging espresso and making sandwiches and I was working the temp job that would eventually lead to a full-time gig. We had become friends over the counter, chatting about music and the weather and his teenage son, then we met for a drink one summer night and talked—to our complete surprise—for six hours.

That friendship and our countless afternoon walks around Cambridge had blossomed into deep love and equally deep feelings of guilt and worry. I knew I was playing with fire by inviting him, but I couldn't imagine a celebration like this without him there.

My birthday fell on a sunny September Saturday, perfect for the casual brunch we had planned. The new minister from our church was the first to arrive, along with a young couple who had caught a ride with her. We chatted in the dining room while my husband flipped stacks of French toast and I poured orange juice and arranged freshly washed berries on the Fiestaware plates we'd gotten for our wedding.

Soon, other voices filled the front hallway: our Jewish friends from Somerville, bearing a bread pudding. The tall, lanky couple who were our first friends in Boston and their 12-year-old twins, who handed me a bouquet of sunflowers as they walked in. And Gamal, nervous at being included in this part of my life but smiling warmly as he wrapped me in a huge hug.

Midway through the party, I found myself alone, pausing in the doorway between the kitchen and dining room. I could hear Gamal's loud laugh and see the twins sprawled on the living room floor, flipping through my magazines. This group of friends—some who knew each other and some who didn't—were chatting and eating, at ease with one another. My friend Ryan had brought a bottle of Champagne and made mimosas. And at one point, everyone had gathered in a circle, smiling, to sing "Happy Birthday."

I still have those Fiestaware plates. But everything else is different now. The collapse didn't happen that day, though it began the next week when a simmering conflict with the minister escalated into a rift with our church community that still hasn't healed. Months later, sitting at the kitchen table with bowls of carrot ginger soup, my husband and I confessed we had each been having affairs. A year after that, as the COVID-19 pandemic upended work and life for millions of Americans, I lost my job after an extended furlough. The life I had known, and had worked so hard to build, is definitely not mine anymore.

I live in a different light-filled apartment now: on a hill in East Boston, near the water, filled with books and houseplants and the trappings of a newly single life. There are signs of another person, too: a framed photo of Gamal and me from last summer up in Salem, a pair of men's size 13 slippers, an extra toothbrush and robe in the bathroom. My divorce gave us the freedom we needed to try out a real relationship—to love each other in the way we couldn't when we were each balancing the other against someone else. We have leaned on each other through loss and joy, and he is both a catalyst for this new life and a fundamental part of it.

My reinvention is still in progress. But on my best days, I believe in the end of Kunitz's poem:

*Though I lack the art*

*to decipher it,*

*no doubt the next chapter*

*in my book of transformations*

*is already written.*

*I am not done with my changes.*

*About the author: Katie Noah Gibson is a writer, runner, flower fiend, cyclist and Texas transplant based in Boston, Massachusetts. She does communications work for a small nonprofit by day and reads all the books by night. www.katieleigh.wordpress.com*

# time for me to fly

By Michael W. Kithcart

We were in his rundown Chrysler in a university village parking lot on the college campus, arguing about my decision to leave for a summer job in another state. "I don't want you to go. I love you," he said.

I unbuckled my seat belt and turned my body in the seat to get a better look at his eyes. He mirrored my actions, so he was facing me. I punched him in the stomach. Hard.

"You have no idea what love is!" I fumed. Not like I had a clue either, but I was sure I knew his motive. "You're just saying that because you don't want me to leave you. You don't really mean it."

He laughed at me. Not in a mocking way, but in an endearing way. "I might not have meant it a minute ago, but I do now. I do love you. Please don't go."

In that moment, a song began to echo loudly in my head. REO Speedwagon's "Time for Me to Fly." I knew I would leave.

In the decades that followed, I was certain "Time for Me to Fly" represented the essence of who I was. Anytime I heard it, I would take it as a sign from the universe that I was supposed to make a change, to take a leap.

It always popped up at exactly the right moment. Randomly

and on purpose. On the car radio, the moment I put the key in the ignition. As I scanned scratchy radio stations while driving in rural areas. Piped into store speakers as I shopped for groceries. Sometimes there would be months or even years when I didn't hear it. Then it would reappear. And with frequency. Once again, a sign it was time to let go of someone or something. Who needed to be out of my life? What job did I need to quit? Where did I need to be living?

"Time for Me to Fly" was my personal reinvention anthem. Each time I evolved into a new version of myself, it represented the end of a relationship. It confirmed what I wasn't going to take anymore. Sung at the top of my lungs, it made me feel empowered. It explained being dumped. It justified moving on. It made me certain that the next partner was destined to be the right one. The presence of the song in my life also meant I didn't need to go deeper in self-examination, to explore what truly didn't work in the relationships. It reinforced the belief that it needed to end.

"Time for Me to Fly" was my professional theme song. When my career weaved in and out of corporate and nonprofit work, failed attempts at government and big leaps to entrepreneurship, my theme song was always with me, reassuring me I'd made the right choice. It convinced me it was the ideal time to take on a big challenge, to apply my experience in a different setting, to pursue a dream. Each new beginning built on the last. And while I'm grateful for every path explored, I wonder now if that theme song drowned out the voice of reason. Did it stop me from seeing that taking flight may have been unnecessary or premature? Had I truly read the situation correctly?

"Time for Me to Fly" was my relocation hymn. Each time I got the itch to move to a new location it confirmed another metamorphosis was underway. When I decided to live in Paris. When I considered relocating to New York City because I said I always wanted to live there. I swear, each of those times, the song was on repeat in my head and everywhere. It convinced me one move was better than the other, to sell all my possessions—homes, cars, furniture. Everything except my books. But did it prevent me from grasping that neither was necessary? That both moves were, in fact, fleeting?

The benefit of time and age is the ability to notice lifelong patterns and to evaluate them both critically and lovingly. Self-discovery has allowed me to finally realize that what I thought was divine intervention via an '80s rock ballad was really me running away—from myself, my fears, my failures. The song was a buffer for extreme discomfort and internal restlessness. Only when I stopped flying was I able to discover what I really wanted out of life.

Learning to ground myself has been painful at times. The realization that everything I ever wanted was right in front of me all along has been humbling. And while initially it was devastating to think I wasted so much time, I know now that each transformation got me closer to my true self emerging. I couldn't have realized the life and career I have now if I hadn't flown so many times, if I hadn't had those experiences that tested me on so many levels.

It took 25 years before I flew back to the man who said he loved me in that beat-up Chrysler. Now I don't ever want to leave him. I'd rather be home living life with him than saying yes to the next city or adventure. He's my biggest champion. I cheer him on to reach new heights. And together we make plans for our future.

When I hear my old anthem now, I still crank it up and sing at the top of my lungs. And then I laugh at myself. "Time for Me to Fly" no longer serves as a signal that something in my life needs to change. I know now I'm exactly where I'm supposed to be, surrounded by people I love, doing exactly what I'm meant to be doing. It also no longer shows up randomly. Maybe the universe is sending signs in different ways. Maybe it's simply not time for me to fly. Or maybe I already am.

*About the author: Michael W. Kithcart is a performance coach for sales leaders, creator of the Wynning Your Way Framework, and podcast host of "Champions of RISK." She champions overstretched sales managers and teams to re-engineer success in a sustainable way, so they win their way in business and life. www.michaelwkithcart.com*

# kintsugi

By Heidi Schneider

The Kintsugi bowl at the Minneapolis Institute of Art is not currently on display, lodging somewhere in the museum's storerooms. The pottery was made in China, thin and delicate with a fluted rim and glazed in a pale jade green color. The inside of the bowl contains an overlapping floral design tenderly etched by the ceramicist, who lived in the 12th or 13th century. The bowl is cracked and repaired with a gold fill. The MIA curator believes it was mended in Japan for a Japanese owner, as Kintsugi was not a Chinese custom.

I remember seeing it displayed years ago, when I took my small children on visits to the museum. "Look at the crack!" I pointed inside the glass case. "Don't you wish you could trace the delicate gold seam with your fingers?" Their eyes lit up at the idea of touching its exquisite beauty, like its owner probably did 700 years ago, after her bowl was returned to her, mended.

My first husband was an artist. He designed our wedding bands in three parts. The top portion was made of rose gold and the bottom portion was yellow gold. In the middle of the ring was a narrow silver ring that was set at an angle, tilting its path through the center and joining the other two pieces together. The symbolism was that we were two separate lives, melding together, but we anticipated both good experiences and difficulties. As one person's strength waned, we hoped the other would compensate with greater vigor. When one person became angry, we hoped the other would grow in love. And we would always make a whole.

A local goldsmith created our rings, which we wore for five years until our divorce. My then-husband lost interest in me as he embraced his own gay identity. No amount of love or strength or forgiveness could keep us whole. The rings were no longer a matched set, but separate, journeying with us as we moved on to new lives and other loves.

For years, I colored my hair to raven brown to hide the gray. Then I stopped. At about the same time I gave up treating my hair, I also gave up wearing makeup, committing fully to looking like the person I am. Sometimes, I still don a little drugstore tiara to crown the ordinary, everyday beauty of aging.

My second husband, Joel, began working full-time from home during the pandemic of 2020. Spending more time in the house, he became increasingly frustrated with the chipped and faded dishes in our kitchen. After several evenings studying china patterns online, he narrowed the selection down to a few choices.

"What do you think of these?" he queried with a quiver of excitement in his voice.

"We really don't need to spend this money right now," I said. "What we have is fine. We are home alone. I can't imagine the next time we will be able to invite guests to our house for dinner."

I failed to say: "I am also resistant to change during periods of stress. Please don't ask me to make this decision."

He nonetheless convinced me that we needed to refresh our kitchen, and new china was the answer. One day, a big box arrived on our doorstep, the contents cheering our home with bold blue stripes on the plates, coffee mugs and bowls.

Joel tossed the chipped pieces of our original set in the trash. I reserved a few damaged plates and bowls because ritual destruction is a valuable tool during a pandemic. Breaking plates can be invigorating for a controlling person like myself. Our son and I broke the first plate in July after he finished an incomplete in one of his college classes following his sheltering-in-place-at-home spring semester online. Another plate was destroyed with joyful abandon after a tense election concluded in the fall. I broke another in celebration of receiving my COVID vaccines. I hold one in reserve for the imminent demise of our beloved golden retriever.

Hurling old china in the driveway and watching it break into sections, big and small, is my privileged suburban method of demonstrating non-attachment and illuminating failure, loss and transition. After the throwing and breaking, I bend over and pick up the china pieces, searching the edge of the driveway for remnants that might puncture a bike tire. Stooping over, acknowledging my own brokenness, salvaging the detritus I created—this is the way of heartbreak, of repentance and of revolution.

My mother likes to say she is "only 96." She refuses to be photographed and does not recognize her own bone-deep beauty. Browsing old yearbooks, she recalls her youth and senses she is now nothing more than a museum piece in storage.

For months, because of the pandemic, we did not see one another at all. The isolation was confusing to her. Her bright smile faded. The witty conversations of the past turned into repeated questions over the phone: "Why can't you come to my apartment? Why don't you visit me anymore?"

As COVID protocols change, I visit with her in her apartment, wearing two masks and a face shield. Although it is difficult to kiss her in my "astronaut gear," as she calls it, I reach out my hand to touch her delicate frame. My hand gently traces her curving spine, through her neatly ironed dress shirt. I am grateful for her precious body, held together with the lacquer of persevering stubbornness and the golden dust of a century of memories.

"What will it be today, Mom? Scrabble, paperwork or cleaning out the closets?" My mother's current obsession is to review every file, every book and every drawer to discard the non-essentials, aiming to achieve a final Zen-like habitation.

"Do you think we have time to play?" She claps her hands like a strict schoolteacher, calling the class to order. "We have so much work to do!"

*About the author: As a child, Heidi Schneider misplaced a diary of original poetry. She is still seeking to recover those lost words. Her writing has been published in Months to Years Magazine, Sleet Magazine, the Together We Carry Project, and the anthology "Choosing Judaism: 36 Stories." www.heidi-schneider.com*

# rock bottom is not the final destination

By Chaz Sandifer

P icture this. Caramel-colored hardwood floors, canary yellow walls, empty white rocking chair swaying in the corner of the room, butterflies decorating the ceiling. I am 32 years old, lying on the floor, sweat dripping, back cramping, spit on my face. My husband just body slammed me on our daughter's bedroom floor. We had an argument about finances, the engagement party I'm headed out of town for, and where the children will stay while we're both out of town in a week. Finances are tight due to the recent recession, and I am the primary provider.

We've been together eight years and he has never put his hands on me in a violent manner. As I lie here in shock, my mind swirls with questions: *Why? What caused his temper to escalate so much that he would physically pick up his wife and slam her to the ground? And how could that her be me?* I am paralyzed with fear, panic and pain. All I hear now are the echoes of his yelling and the stomping of his feet pacing back and forth on the hard floor.

*How am I going to get up and get out? Where is my phone?* My head is throbbing. Ten minutes pass, but it feels like hours. He's in the bathroom when my phone rings. I manage to pick it up and hear a friend say, "Hey girl, what are we doing tonight?" Her voice is a blessing. She is prompting me, through my uncontrollable tears, to explain what happened.

"Grab your keys to your car and run," she says with clarity and authority.

*Is this really happening? Am I really going to run from my own husband and my house?* But that's exactly what I do. I make my way to my car and drive down the street. No shoes, no bra, no coat. After a few minutes, I pull over to catch my breath; my friend stays on the phone and tries to calm me. All I can think now is *thank God my babies weren't home*.

In an instant, everything has changed. My trust in men, my faith in this life, my purpose and drive to move forward — it has all left me. I thought I'd been a good wife and mother. Now I didn't know what I was. I didn't know who the hell I married. I would never look at him the same. *Don't come by me, don't look at me. Your apologies, cards and flowers mean nothing.* Days passed and I didn't speak to him. Not once. I boarded a plane and headed to my friend's engagement party as planned.

When I came back, we fell into our old patterns. He did everything he could to get things back to where they'd been. We took our annual family trip to Wisconsin Dells and had weekly date nights. But deep down, I felt hate for him. Soon the fights started again, but with me as the aggressor and name caller. I wanted him to feel what it was like to be the victim.

Eight months later, I found myself being chased around the dining room table. I ran into the laundry room. As he charged at me, I slipped on a pile of laundry and fell. He slapped my leg so hard it felt like he'd cut me. He balled his fist, pulled it back and stopped. He screamed, "I'm not gonna hit you, you stupid bitch!" Fearing for my life, I grabbed a butcher knife. I looked down and realized what I was about to do. My hand was shaking. I dropped the knife. I grabbed my purse and the kids and headed to my parents' house. I knew I would never be back.

The next three long and stressful years of separation included restraining orders and court cases. Broken hearts and egos. Lost souls. At 35 years old, I found myself 40 pounds overweight and drinking two bottles of wine a night. It was my rock bottom. I felt like I'd been buried alive and couldn't get out. I didn't want to be a mother, a sister or a friend. I didn't want to exist at all.

Then, one night, I was sitting in the living room of my townhouse while the kids were playing. There was pizza on the table and juice boxes on the floor. I began to cry for no reason and every reason. My son looked at me and came to sit on my lap. He grabbed my cheeks and pulled my face close to his. "Mommy, you're so pretty," he said, looking directly into my eyes. "But you're kind of a fat chunky chunk."

He wasn't just referring to my physical appearance; he saw that I was broken. My spirit was broken. Other people had voiced concerns as well. But I couldn't see where I truly was in life until I saw it through my son's eyes.

I decided to stop drinking. I vowed to work out every morning for 30 days and lost 15 pounds. I became a bodybuilder so I could be strong on all levels. I went to counseling to work on myself and figure out what I was going to do about my marriage. There was one thing left to do. I called my husband from outside of his work and told him to come out; we needed to talk in person.

"What the *eff* do you want?" he asked when he walked up to my vehicle.

"I forgive you and I forgive myself," I said.

"Why?" he asked as tears began to flow from his eyes.

"I have no hate left in my heart for you," I said.

With those words, I released the pain I'd been holding. I was finally able to move forward. I filed for divorce. He was devastated. But on March 11, 2013, I walked out of the courtroom with my head held high and my dignity back.

I went on to compete in my first bodybuilding figure competition, unconcerned about where I finished. I had already beaten the odds and came out ahead. I became a certified life and wellness coach and a group fitness instructor; bought the Camden Farmers Market, which I'd been managing for two years; and then launched theNEWmpls, a health and wellness company that guides women with a holistic approach.

I've learned so many lessons during my journey: Forgive yourself and others who've caused you pain. Walk in your light and follow your passion. Prayers and time heal everything. Tell your story so no one else can. But perhaps the biggest: Rock bottom is not the final destination.

*About the author: Chaz Sandifer is the CEO and founder of theNEWmpls, a Minneapolis, Minnesota-based company dedicated to affordable fitness, wellness and nutrition. Bringing her holistic approach to the community, Chaz breaks generational cycles of poor health by instilling that fitness is fun, quality nutrition is essential, and wellness is key to a healthy future. www.thenewmpls.info*

# blue dresses

By Cynthia Lehew-Nehrbass

A box of blue polyester dance dresses slides around the back of my Jeep, hitting the sides with dull thuds. Amazon awaits its UPS store return—return codes issued, accounts credited. For three months the dresses have frozen and unfrozen in my trunk. Bags of groceries, snowshoes, suitcases and dog food have rested on top of them. They've passed by the UPS store several times, sat outside for 15 minutes once, but never found their way inside. Why? Because they almost danced at my mother's funeral.

"Don't wear black at mine," Mom said, hands on hips, as if I'd be the only one in the room that mattered. Not my cousins, younger sister or several dozen other mourners who'd all be wearing black. Just me. "It's so depressing."

I hardly reacted. I refused to respond with a typical guffaw or a sarcastic, "Oh, you know I will," like every funeral we'd attended before. Every single one.

Yes, I admit I own way too much black. Years and years of it. Dancing black, butt-flattering black, discount rack and rummage sale black. And, of course, I'm wearing black pants as I write this. But the slacks are slimming (she would appreciate this), from a clearance rack (such a deal!) and can be worn to teach my son's college dance team (so practical!).

"Dance to this like you did for Grandma's," my 80-year-old mom said as her favorite hymn, "On Eagle's Wings," played. Oh, she knew I would bawl like I did at both my grandparents' services and the one for my dear friend's daughter. She must have pictured it so clearly. My controlled turns, ballet extensions, the wet-faced sniffles. And she knew I owned a whole dance company's worth of Martha Graham-style long black skirts used for decades of Good Friday services. She was worried I would wear my lacrymosa one for her "day of tears." She knew I knew this too. With a raised brow and her eyes' teasing twinkle, she reiterated, "But don't wear black."

So, how many dresses does it take to be able to dance at your mother's funeral? How many shades of blue? Bell sleeves or angel wings? Calf length or ruffles to the floor? Is it royal or navy, perhaps periwinkle, or deep sapphire that can make the day less excruciating, your feet able to point, your leg to lift, your lungs to exhale without sobbing, your arms to grab the air toward heaven to pull her back down to earth again? How many damn dresses does it take?

Apparently six. Almost nine, but the last three were back-ordered and never showed up. Four different sizes, tight waist and bosom covering, baggy hipped and crew necked, some with a triangular scarf. Son and son's girlfriend each had their favorite. So did husband. Petite daughter could have fit into one. But the very first to arrive, deep royal, the truest of blues, Mom's eye color in the shadow of dark, was the one selected in the end. All the others, on the night before her funeral, were hung, dejected, in the guestroom. The room where I went to hide and curl under the blanket Mom had been covered in after she died.

The blanket was blue too. Not completely so, with some white and a pretty peachy beige. I bought it for Mom when she was in rehab recovering from hip surgery. And it was so soft. Mom loved soft things. She was always covered with it. For her vigil of TV watching, her restless recliner sleeping, even when her body was purple and cold. When I crawled into bed next to her, put my head on her shoulder as she laid unmoving, sans breath, and rested my hand on her still gurgling tummy.

The blanket smelled like her. Mom's smell. A lotion-layered dry skin scent mixed with her favorite foamy soap. Her neck, the sweat she had from not showering recently, that too. Strangely, unclean Mom smelled better to me. Mom's armpit, Mom's belly that housed her womb, my first home. And the slight decay of her empty shell, alone for the many hours before we knew she was gone. It was all there in the blanket. I would never let anyone touch it and wondered how long the smell of life and death would linger there. When the threads of the fabric would finally let go of Mom too and become again just a blanket. I prayed never.

If I could have danced in that blanket, I would have. Stitched it into something wearable, some type of ritual funeral garment, with elastic and straps from old leotards. Then I would have had the scent of Mom on me with every pirouette, torso twist, signed gestures to the phrases: *Raise you up. Eagle's wings. Breath of God. Rock in whom I trust.*

But in the end, I chose the first dress that was ordered from a photo on my phone and two days later was plopped onto my doorstep by a stranger. It was perfect for that day. People said it was as if Mom had chosen it herself. When I danced her home, those few moments my arms searched for her and lifted her up, she was with me in wherever heaven on earth might be. We were in a space together one more time, her and I.

So how many dresses does it take to dance at your mother's funeral? The one that you are in at the time.

All the others, I will keep. In my trunk they will remain until I tire of hearing them behind me with every direction turn and every hill climbed. Until I become brave enough in my grief to deal with them. Then they will hang, side by side, on velvet hangers in my basement cedar closet, next to the chosen dress, my lacrymosa skirts, the finally arrived back-ordered dresses and maybe my imaginary blanket dress. Because that row of mourning is where they ultimately belong.

*About the author: Cynthia Lehew-Nehrbass is a Minneapolis, Minnesota-based writer, professional dancer/choreographer/teacher, certified health coach, special needs parent and advocate, pastor's wife, and proud mom of two young adults. Her writing is found in many anthologies and publications. When not busy creating or teaching, she enjoys kayaking, long walks and time with family.*

# goodwill hunting

By Leslie Lagerstrom

U p until a year ago, I would not have been caught dead in a thrift store. My assessment of Goodwill and similar establishments was that they were smelly places where dirty, used, outdated clothes and housewares went to die. A last stop before the landfill that only hoarders frequented because they were the lone ones who could perceive value in what I thought was trash.

But then my son Sam started a side hustle selling on eBay and insisted some of the best places to find merchandise were these caverns of gloom. For months, he pleaded with me to join him. Every time he did, my answer was a swift and indignant NO. Until one day, he wore me down with a carefully crafted argument that can only be described as nagging mixed with guilt. I reluctantly tagged along—traipsing 10 feet behind with my T-shirt pulled over my nose to emphasize my aversion. I think back on that day with embarrassment for the blatant conceit I displayed. And because I could not have been more wrong.

To my surprise, these stores—we have five favorites in the Twin Cities metro area and one just across the Minnesota border—are filled with absolute gems. It's true, beauty is in the eye of the beholder, but it can also be found in the carefully trained eye of an eBay reseller who knows just what to look for. With Sam as my mentor, I learned this type of shopping is like going on a treasure hunt. It's an exhilarating trip into unknown waters, where I almost always emerge with some sort of loot—either for Sam's business or for myself (the latter being frowned upon by Sam, who constantly reminds me that we are running a business, not outfitting my home).

Now Sam and I hit these stores together on a regular basis. We know the best days and times to shop to maximize our bounty (Mondays and Tuesdays, in case you were wondering). Since turning 55, I'm considered a senior citizen, so on Wednesdays I receive a 20 percent discount. I could not be more thrilled. *Who am I and what happened to the old me?* I often wonder as I peruse my favorite aisles with a rickety-wheeled shopping cart that not so subtly signals to other shoppers to get the hell out of my way. Competitiveness has taken the place of embarrassment as my skills mature.

As weeks of thrifting have turned into months, I have earned a graduate-level education—not only about thrifting, but about myself.

In the beginning, I thought it called for being discreet. I didn't want to appear as a picker (a shopper who aggressively scoops up good deals for resale without regard to others). That lasted no more than a week. I realized almost all shoppers are pickers and therefore competition. Now, I think nothing of shouting down the aisles while hoisting a coveted prize in the air, "Sam! I think this will be easy to flip!"

Lessons in thrifting etiquette have taught me it's in poor taste to reach over someone's shoulder to seize merchandise for oneself. I learned this the hard way from a woman whose elbow accidentally connected with my ribs while I stretched to grab a piece of Wedgwood. It turns out, it's also not polite to block large sections of display racks with your cart, thereby rendering them unavailable to others. Although I must admit, if I feel anxious about the number of shoppers in a particular section, I have sometimes employed this tactic. *Do as I say, not as I do.*

What I have learned about myself has been even more revelatory. I never knew finding matching sets of plates and bowls from Pottery Barn, Crate and Barrel, and Ralph Lauren (the granddaddy of them all!) could make me so giddy. I've found happiness in the sustainability aspect of thrifting as well. The need to bring my own newspaper to pack fragile purchases has prompted me to restart my subscription to the local paper. Recycling that paper allows me to offer yet another nod to the environment. No more pretending for this old gal—I now consider myself the "Queen of Green."

Recycling is just one of the ways resourcefulness shows up in my thrifting endeavors. When going on family road trips, I schedule pit stops along the way that coincide with towns where the best thrift stores are located. Feigning ignorance only worked the first couple of breaks for gas and food, and then my family was onto me. Now I fully own it. "Where there is a Goodwill, there is a way!" has become my mantra when my husband insists there is no extra room in the car to accommodate my purchases.

Readiness is key when it comes to thrifting. Always prepared for the expedition ahead, I arrive bright and early and armed with reading glasses, a phone for checking prices and a cross-body purse to keep my hands free. This allows me to fully enjoy being in my element and to experience the adrenaline rush that comes from finding a Tiffany trinket box hidden behind a bunch of melted candles. Or a vintage Scooby-Doo lunchbox under a pile of board games with missing pieces. Though sometimes, the adrenaline comes later. Sam and I recently purchased a simple white ceramic birdhouse, which we hoped to flip for a few bucks. Turns out it was a unicorn—an early production piece from a popular artist that was originally sold at a local big box retailer. We ended up selling it for $1,997 more than we paid. The profit was thrilling, but the bragging rights that came from finding something so rare were even better.

Upon reflection, this journey has been more than just a change in attitude. Rather, it's a midlife metamorphosis. I went from never stepping into a thrift shop to being a proud card-carrying member of the VIP Frequent Buyer's Club. Thrifting allows me to let my hair down, literally and figuratively. After 20 years in corporate America, where I constantly worried about deadlines, management demands and conforming to a cubicle mentality, I am free to be me in all my shopping glory. My biggest worry these days is whether I'll arrive in time to beat the other regular shoppers to the china and crystal aisle.

The independence is exhilarating. The challenge invigorating. This is the new me with a fresh sense of purpose.

*About the author: Leslie Lagerstrom is an advocate for transgender children and their families. Her writing is featured in four anthologies, including "Chicken Soup for the Soul," and has been made into a stage production. A proud mom of two, Leslie lives in Minnesota, where she enjoys hiking with her husband and dogs.*

# stirred not shaken

By Kathleen Foye MacLennan

In my mid-30s, I found myself dreading social situations where I had to answer the inevitable question, *what do you do?* Trying to embrace my new role of corporate wife, mother and now nonprofit community volunteer (a title I loathed), I struggled to answer. Searching for relevance, I signed up for a spiritual gifts seminar.

I'd just returned from living overseas with my young family. A feisty trial attorney by trade, I took a few years off intending to return to the courtroom once stateside. The birth of my third child coupled with my husband's travel prompted me to decide to stay home. This seminar was going to be my silver bullet to give my life new meaning and direction—it was like cheap therapy and professional coaching, with a little God mixed in.

Sadly, the seminar silver bullet was eluding me. I felt like I was transported back to high school struggling to solve those confounding Algebra II word problems where the trains start at different points and you calculate the rate of travel and determine when they cross paths. I seriously never got one of those correct. I always prayed to the god of partial credit during the test.

So here I was again, praying to that same god. My life resembled two trains barreling away from each other. I wasn't going back to work, but where was I going? Sensing my exasperation, the young minister pulled up his chair, looking eager to unlock my potential. After three hours of self-analysis and testing, I still could not identify my spiritual gift that we all supposedly possess.

"Where do you feel you are at your best?" the minister asked. Sensing my paralysis, he asked the question a different way. "When do you shine?"

"At a cocktail party!" I blurted out without regard to my holy audience. A little mortified, but it was the God's honest truth.

Without flinching, the minister concluded, "You have the gift of hospitality."

I recoiled. Hospitality? It conjured up my inner Hillary Clinton. *What am I supposed to do? Stay home and bake cookies and stand by my man?* I wanted my gift to be wisdom or, better yet, leadership. My gift was not serving people like some biblical Martha (she was uptight) versus Mary (who was more chill). Hospitality just seemed like a nice way to say housewife or deferential to men.

"Why is the cocktail party the place where you feel good, other than the buzz, of course?" the minister quipped.

I told him I genuinely liked people and was a master at playing who-do-we-mutually-know bingo. I knew how to work the room. It felt natural to me to ask personal questions and have folks share their very intimate answers. More importantly, I knew how to put people at ease. I curated and connected people based on their backgrounds, interests and ideas. I knew how to weave people together and then take myself out of the equation. I brought folks together for their benefit, not mine.

When we moved overseas, I hit it hard. It was me who connected the whole family to our community. I taught my Syrian neighbors to carve pumpkins for Halloween and organized a make-your-own Valentine's party for my befuddled Swedish friends. I hosted dinner parties where 12 different nationalities debated controversial topics without causing political hangovers.

Looking back, in talking with the minister, I actually described a type of hospitality, but oddly I couldn't see it. I left the seminar feeling unenlightened and a little pissed off.

But the hostess label lingered and haunted me as I redefined my life and career. Slowly and for the first time, I began to realize the difference between being good at something due to skill (law) and being good at something because you are wired that way (gift). It was an epiphany—being available for others comes easy to me.

Hospitality was not just events and entertaining; it was constantly collecting people and spotting challenges and opportunities. Hospitality included matching resources with needs and skills. Service with much more than just a smile. It dawned on me that I'm wired to find the strengths in others, to see the potential and connect the dots. Finally, I understood that hospitality is a mindset that makes things possible. Hospitality is persuading others to come along with me.

In my work for nonprofits, I bring the same focus and creativity to the boardroom as I do to the cocktail party. I recruit others, wooing them into a project that matches their interests and comfort level. I'm often the spark and the informal director of creating impactful partnerships and initiatives.

My gift is even more apparent when I mentor under-resourced high school students. To ease nerves, I reignite my overseas food tricks, offering ample Halloween candy or a Valentine's Day cookie. With this crowd, hospitality means humbly listening and figuring out how to move forward together. Talking with some students is like seeking and finding the most uncomfortable person at the party, staying engaged in the conversation as a sort of lifeline, and making the moment a little less lonely or painful. It means sticking with them through the labyrinth of college applications, financial aid, scholarships and job applications, nurturing confidence and celebrating next steps.

Now I welcome the question, *what do you do?*

"I'm a connector," I say proudly. "My gift is hospitality."


*About the author: Kathleen Foye MacLennan attributes her love of storytelling to her childhood, being the seventh of eight in a boisterous Catholic household. Every day she tries to put pen to paper to capture the humorous and humbling moments of her life as a former litigation attorney, mother, wife and volunteer.*

# courage, growth and transformation

By Michelle Tran Maryns

My parents were part of the first wave of refugees who immigrated to the United States in 1975. They settled in a small farming community in Kansas that had a large KKK contingency. We were one of the few families of color in that town. While I am eternally grateful for the many amazing people who welcomed and helped my family start anew in the U.S. when we had nothing, I also have shadows and memories of being visited by people who clearly did not want us to be there. We stayed inside a lot and didn't answer the door for fear of who or what might be outside.

When I was older, my dad got a better paying job in a bigger town. But the discrimination didn't stop there. Men at my dad's factory used to throw trash on the floor for fun and tell him to pick it up, even though it was not part of his job description and he technically held the same position as them.

My mom came to this country without her high school degree. When I was young, I helped her study for and ultimately earn her GED, and I was proud to help her get a decent paying job as an assembler. She endured sexual harassment from her supervisor in that job. Seeing the stark contrast between a self-determined mom who owned a successful fabric business back in Vietnam and the one who suffered harassment at a job that was both physically and emotionally harmful broke my heart.

As a young person, I felt both frustrated and powerless that I couldn't do more to help my parents end the humiliation and harassment they experienced. As a student who looked different from my classmates and could not afford the things that might help me fit in more, I experienced bullying myself. I studied and worked as hard as I possibly could, determined to help end the anguish of my family and others in my community.

I inherited my mom's entrepreneurial spirit and filled notebooks with all of my business ideas. In middle school, I learned about a program for young people interested in business. I signed up and won a trip to New York City to visit the New York Stock Exchange and NASDAQ. It was my first time in a city of that size and I loved it. We stayed at the New York Athletic Club, which the New York Times in 1989 reported was a "club [that] had voluntarily agreed to end the two-year legal battle it had waged to remain a male bastion." I was the only female on the trip, but I thought I blended in because I was wearing a suit. Later, when a driver assumed I was the wife of one of the investment bankers in our group, I realized that was not the case.

Toward the end of the trip, my mentor said he thought I was too nice and not tough enough to be in the business world. I was confused because I had worked hard and my portfolio spoke for itself. I didn't think I acted differently from the other student on the trip, and

I didn't hear anyone telling him he was too nice to be in the business world. I later learned that other femme entrepreneurs were told similar things when they started.

Looking back, I realize that "too nice" might have been code for a lot of things. Asian women are often stereotyped as being quiet and submissive. The most ironic thing about this stereotype is that like my mom and many Asian women I know, I am not a quiet or submissive person. I may not always shout, take up too much space, offend or act aggressively, but I definitely speak my mind. And my mom comes from a long line of very powerful Asian women. Like the Trưng sisters and Lady Triệu, who actually rode elephants and led armies of people to fight off those attempting to conquer their land. In fact, scholars think Vietnam was once a matriarchal society.

I cared for my mother-in-law, another strong and powerful woman, during the last few years of her life. It opened my eyes to the fact that our time here on earth is just too short to let others dim your light or dull your sparkle. It became my mantra: *Let your light shine and help others shine so that together we sparkle.* The resilience and toughness that both my mom and my mother-in-law showed despite the adversity they were dealt in life, combined with this mantra, gave me the courage to finally start my own business, We Sparkle, a public benefit corporation building a stronger and more inclusive economy by equipping underestimated entrepreneurs with the AI-powered tools they need to succeed.

According to Brené Brown, "Courage starts with showing up and letting ourselves be seen ... The root of the word courage is cor— the Latin word for heart. In one of its earliest forms, the word courage meant to speak one's mind by telling all one's heart." For me that means even if one's heart is broken. Perhaps for me that is the only way I may be able to heal and mend after many years of heartache.

I am grateful to everyone who has inspired me by being courageous and sharing their own stories as they are able and for showing up in countless other ways for those who need support.

*About the author: Michelle Tran Maryns is founder and CEO of We Sparkle Co., a Techstars-backed public benefit corporation building a stronger and more inclusive economy by equipping underestimated entrepreneurs with the AI-powered software tools they need to succeed. www.wesparkle.co*

# exorcism of the exhausted mother

By Heidi Fettig Parton

I made my way along a late February sidewalk, trying to stay balanced on a thin glaze of ice. Walking the five blocks between my house and the energy healer's office, I kept thinking about what my first yoga teacher used to say: Seek balance, not stability.

I'd been harboring apprehension about this, my first visit to an energy healer. Was this a part of the occult world my mom used to warn about? In the sixth grade, I convinced my friend Laura to let me burn her Ouija board in the alley behind her house. I'd overheard my mom's friend saying "The Exorcist" was based on a true story about a boy who became possessed by demons after he'd played with a Ouija board.

By then, I already knew too much about "The Exorcist." Two years earlier, my oldest brother—not quite a hands-on sitter— was charged with my care one Saturday night. He spent the evening watching TV in our basement family room, which was directly below my bedroom. After putting myself to bed, I heard that now recognizably haunting piano music penetrating my bedroom vents. Unable to sleep, I ventured downstairs to get my brother to turn down the volume. He sat on a beanbag in front of the TV in the darkened room. After taking a swig of Mello Yello he asked, "What's your problem, kid?"

I didn't answer because I was watching a girl's head spinning on the TV. Terrified of returning upstairs alone, I backed up to the couch and pulled a crocheted blanket around me. If my brother knew I was there, he didn't send me away. He didn't know I'd spend the next 11 months sleeping with my bedroom light on; I couldn't let go of the fear that I too might become possessed. I was an anxious child who grew into an anxious adult.

By the time I sought out the energy healer, I'd been trapped in my house for eight months—since my third child, Josh, had undergone a delicate ear surgery. My singular mission was to prevent his exposure to any illness that might jeopardize his healing—even the common cold was a threat. I lived in constant fear of disease-causing bacteria and viruses.

Josh's ear surgery had unseated the fragile sense of stability I'd negotiated since his birth three years earlier. Mere hours after birth, he'd been diagnosed with congenital hearing loss. At 10 months, an audiologist fit Josh with hearing aids. They miraculously worked and he began to slowly acquire spoken language.

Two years later, Josh required surgery to repair a damaged right eardrum. The surgery unexpectedly revealed the reason for his conductive hearing loss—underdeveloped middle ear bones. In the middle of the surgery, the ENT left the OR to ask us for permission to replace our son's first two ear bones with a small titanium rod. We reluctantly agreed to what we'd later learn was an ossicular chain reconstruction. The surgery restored our son's hearing, but an ear infection could threaten both his new eardrum and the prosthesis that had given Josh the ability to hear unaided.

For eight months, I'd been carrying around a heavy ball of worry as if it were a shield to ward off danger, as if worrying might prove a preventative action. By then, the restoration seemed both blessing and curse. Like the Tolkien character Gollum, Josh's restored hearing had become "my precious." With my mental and physical health unraveling, I booked an appointment with an energy healer named Trudy who officed near my Saint Paul, Minnesota home.

When I arrived at Trudy's office after successfully navigating the icy sidewalks, I removed one of my woolen mittens to punch in the access code next to her name on the office directory. After she buzzed me inside, I climbed a dimly lit flight of stairs to the landing where Trudy herself, a broad-shouldered woman with cropped gray hair, welcomed me.

Once seated on a nubby tweed sofa in Trudy's office, her dog—a small brindled terrier—jumped up beside me. I scratched behind his ears, warming my cold fingers as he curled into a sleeping ball by my side. For the first time in months, I felt my body relax. *Someone is going to take care of me today.*

"Tell me why you're here," Trudy said. I was more than willing to tell her everything I knew about how I'd gotten to that stuck, scared place in life, even the part about resenting my husband because he had the luxury of venturing off to work, leaving the house and the worry behind. The large woman listened to me with her whole body and when I finished my story, she looked me directly in the eye. "My dear," she said. "You have a bad case of Exhausted Mother's Syndrome. Your son will be okay. Now, you need to take care of yourself."

I carried Trudy's words with me as I walked home in the bluish light of a late winter dusk. I promised myself I'd take action.

Before the first sitter I'd hired all year left my home, I set up a schedule for her to come back regularly so I could attend a yoga class. Then, I started leaving my husband with our son on Saturday mornings so I could escape to coffee shops and write a little bit and—more importantly—enjoy a few much-needed hours of feeling like a regular person.

The exorcism of my demons didn't come all at once, but by the end of that first session, Trudy had already convinced me that if I wanted to find my way to healing, I needed to let go of my tight-fisted grasp on Josh's restored, yet fragile, hearing. I needed to let go, not to survive—I was doing that—but to thrive and to have something other than fear to offer my young, beautiful son.

*About the author: Heidi Fettig Parton received an MFA in creative nonfiction from Bay Path University after retiring from a distinguished legal career. Heidi's writing can be found in many publications, including Brevity, Entropy, The Forge Literary Magazine, Multiplicity Magazine, Saint Paul Almanac, The Manifest-Station and The Rumpus. www.heidifettigparton.com*

# finding my way back

By Jody Vallee Smith

When I was 13, my parents gave me tickets to a Depeche Mode concert at Dodger Stadium in Los Angeles. Flooded with nothing but hormones and brooding independence, I delighted in the fact that I was about to spend my first unsupervised evening with friends. This event called for something special. A box of hair dye and a bottle of nail polish was all it took. To my mother's chagrin, the girl who went to bed the night before was not the same one who walked out of the bathroom 10 minutes before the show. Black lace, blue eyeliner, dark purple hair, zinc pink lips and black fingernails. It was my first reinvention.

A decade later, on the heels of a destructive relationship with a tattooed narcissist, I reinvented myself again. This time, I slid into the requisite cadence of life and the checking of boxes: get a college degree, meet and marry a nice boy, buy a house, have kids. My soul's desire to fight the status quo was still strong. It no longer showed up as purple hair, but it was there. During his toast at my wedding, my dad quipped, "I thought she would bring home a man with tattoos. Turns out, she's the one with the tattoos." I continued to propel myself forward on the moving walkway known as The American Dream, building a life and family in the Arizona desert.

A decade after that, I reinvented myself as the owner of a successful interior design business in Scottsdale. Caught in the blur of entrepreneurship along with caring for two young children and managing a home in the suburbs, I found myself vacillating between coffee and chardonnay. I was still busy checking off boxes: be a good parent to my babies, check in on my own parents, make time for my husband, get to the bottom of my incessant dizziness every morning. The exhaustion and brain fog I experienced on a daily basis had become debilitating. A neurologist diagnosed me with multiple sclerosis. Thankfully, it turned out to be a misdiagnosis. But my body, my therapist and my inner perfectionist all conceded it would be best to close up shop and slow down my life.

My husband's Minnesota birthplace had been a constant whisper for years. The idea of living in the northern Midwest was not one my Southern California roots were too interested in exploring. And yet, sometimes reinvention involves opening yourself up to possibilities outside of your comfort zone. So we moved to Minneapolis, where my next reinvention transpired.

The pace of my old life as a full-time working mom became a blur. I got comfortable in my new surroundings. I devoted the next decade to my daughters. I carpooled. I PTA'd. I chaperoned. I led school activities. And then I felt a different kind of longing. Midlife was no longer the land of box-checking. Women in their 40s were recalibrating, reclaiming the parts of themselves they gave up for others or for the sake of happy keeping. My soul was calling for reinvention, but not like before. It was louder this time, more intense. I needed to fill the hole Gabor Maté calls "the hungry ghost." But how would I fill a hole I didn't consciously remember emptying?

I couldn't hear what my inner voice was telling me. But I knew she was longing to explore and grow and evolve. So I stopped. I got super quiet. I read every book I could get my hands on about wild women, the heroine's journey and pleasure. I explored the underworld with a shaman. I had my chakra graph painted. My soul language and soul animal were identified. I retreated into mindfulness and meditation. I put crystals in my bra. I wrote a children's book about a princess who was the opposite of a damsel in distress. I created enough vision boards to fill Dodger Stadium. I studied Tarot and pulled cards every day for a year. Ironically, what I didn't do was find myself.

In Tarot, the Temperance card is said to represent balance, moderation, patience and purpose. It wasn't until I heard the word used in relation to sword-making that I fully understood it. To temper a sword is to put it directly into the fire to heat it, and then into water to cool it, over and over again. This process keeps the strength of the sword intact, while simultaneously softening it, making it less brittle. You place the sword INTO the fire to make it strong and flexible. I began to think that perhaps reinvention is like temperance. Spending decades walking into the fire, taking risks, changing again and again, knowing your heart and soul may be reshaped but doing it anyway because you will come out of it tougher and more resilient.

My now 13- and 16-year-old girls provide daily reminders that reinvention isn't always complicated. I marvel watching them come into their own—in their own ways and in ways that are reminiscent of that purple-haired girl at the Depeche Mode concert all those years ago. Seeing them transform before my eyes reminds me that reinvention is often just a new look, a new attitude, a readiness to take on the world, an eagerness to embrace what's next. I am realizing that perhaps reinvention is not about finding yourself at all. Perhaps it's about finding your way back to who you've always been and having the courage to be that person in the world.

*About the author: Jody Vallee Smith is a writer, children's book author and magic maker residing just outside of Minneapolis, Minnesota. Her storytelling is inspired by her teenage daughters, who navigate the world using their imagination, grit, smarts and whimsy. Jody believes compassion, humor and a little more play can change the world.*

# dancing with words

By Lisa Harris

T he words danced in solitude to the loneliness of my heart. Yes, they danced. Words don't dance, you say? To a poet, they most certainly do. For as long as I can remember, they have danced for me. Their beauty hypnotic, their vulnerability frightening. These dancing words were my constant and loyal companions in a never-ending search for safety and love. And yet, for over two decades, they danced in secret spaces behind locked doors.

I longed to break them free. But before this could happen, I needed to face her. She was familiar with the dance. She was the 15-year-old girl within me. I had abandoned her for 20 years. Now, happiness and well-being were dependent on rekindling our love.

I found her, just as I remembered, standing on the front step of our childhood home, wishing on a star and extending her hand. This time, I would not turn away. I reached for her and pulled her into a tight embrace. So close, she became an extension of me. In between the murmur of our quiet sobs, I consoled her and whispered, "Please forgive me. You are safe now."

She was an old soul, as the elders would say. Her shy and confident demeanor fascinated those who met her. The softness in her eyes spoke to their very soul. *She was magic*. That was before the world saw her body as their property and her silence as submission. That was before he took away her innocence and her trust. When that happened, from that moment forward, she lived many false realities.

As a mother, I knew she needed me. I could feel it in my womb, the way only mothers can feel the pain of their child from across a crowded room. I wanted to blanket her in love and protect her, but I did not know how. At 35 years old, I was just becoming reacquainted with the 15-year-old girl I had left behind. Neither of us knew the unraveling of self that would transpire in the years to come as I danced with words, displayed them and invited others to join me.

In 2010, after walking away from a 13-year corporate career and executive title, I released the words from the dark spaces in my mind and allowed them to dance on blank pages. Calling it creative expression, I weaved the words together in poetic verse, exposing the shadows and tempting the light. What was I thinking? Was I really going to share them with the world? *Keep these words to yourself. Be an obedient child. Keep your shameful secrets hidden.* Then, in a corner booth at a restaurant in our hometown, my high school girlfriend read my poetry. She embraced 15-year-old me. She spoon-fed me the courage required to push forward.

Six years later, on the last night of an unseasonably cold September, my newly published poetry book took center stage at a launch event in Minneapolis, Minnesota. The book had become the dance floor where I unlocked my words and allowed them to dance.

It provided a platform for powerful healing and growth. But not just my own. At numerous poetry readings and book signings across the country, women approached me to share their personal stories too. It was no longer about me; it was about them.

The book inspired live storytelling events for women. At these events, I watched courageous women share their stories, hold back and release their tears, and reclaim their power. All of the stories were different, but all of the women shared a similar loneliness and strength. In a room full of new acquaintances and old friends, it became evident that none of us were strangers. We were all dancers of a similar dance. We were connected by words and stories.

The night I stepped onto the stage and shared my own story, I experienced the transformative power and healing of storytelling. In that moment, the words freed me, and being witnessed was a gift to my soul. I finally knew how to love her, my 15-year-old self. Her trauma did not define her. Her worthiness was not dependent on someone else's love or approval. After all, she was already magic.

From that moment on, it became my mission to help other women shift their narratives and rewrite their stories. The stories we tell and how we tell them become our reality and give life meaning. If we begin to see words and stories as bridges and remedies for the soul, we can address the wounds of our hearts and the world we live in.

My words still dance. Sometimes they are alone, but they are no longer lonely. They are unafraid to be seen in daylight. Thirty years later, my 15-year-old self and my words rejoice in a celebratory dance of acceptance, peace and self-love.

*In the distance, I see a radiant light peeking from underneath the door.*

*I hear the music.*

*I have the key.*

*Don't be afraid.*

*I can teach your words how to dance.*

*Shall we?*

*About the author: Lisa Harris is a storyteller and narrative coach who helps women reclaim their personal power through the lens of their own life stories. Her entrepreneurial journey began after publishing her book, "Unveiled Beauty: Handwritten Stories From a Poetic Heart." Previously, Lisa worked in leadership roles at Fortune 500 companies. www.lisaharrisandco.com*

# invisible cape with no superpowers

By Kim Kane

I t felt like it happened within seconds. Just like that, my opinions and suggestions did not seem important. I had worked in the field of education for close to 34 years, 24 of them in one district, and 17 in the same building. And within what seemed like a flick of a switch, I sensed I was not valuable anymore. Not wanted anymore. I knew my strengths were refined, my capabilities strong. I was seasoned enough to know when to step in and when to allow others to lead and not personalize the outcomes. Most importantly, I loved my work. So, what changed? The answer is very simple and very complicated ... it was my age.

It became apparent when I started working with a new supervisor. A new supervisor who was younger than my oldest son. While I had reservations about his experience and abilities, I also knew it's about who you surround yourself with that creates the good work. I knew he had many strong, very capable people surrounding him. I had worked with many of them for several years as a team, and we knew and embraced the strengths each person brought to the table. I also believed that supporting leaders is about supporting the work. However, what I never expected—what I never saw coming—were his reservations about *my* experience and abilities. In fact, out of all the concerns, it was something I had never considered.

It started in small ways. I was no longer asked for my input regarding changes or for the sharing of new ideas, yet he repeatedly asked if I'd completed my work without any trouble. Was I able to keep up? A new emotion while at work reared its ugly head for me: feeling insulted. He addressed everyone else in meetings before me. Others on my team were being asked for information in spite of me being the team lead. I became invisible. I became insignificant. In a short amount of time, I was silently being told I was no longer needed. I met this silence with silence. I lost my voice. I lost who I was.

Overall, I am not a loud person, but I pride myself on using my voice for those I serve. I see big pictures and I like to help connect the dots and create the whys for all to understand. Thus, when I started to realize I could no longer connect the dots on why I wasn't included or valued in my work, I lost my balance. I lost my stride. It seemed the only uniqueness I offered was being the oldest in the room. I was hurt, suddenly embarrassed and uncomfortable with my age, and I continued to feel invisible. I felt like I was wearing an invisible cape that I could not take off. And this particular cape held no superpowers.

I realize looking back that I began to question my skill set. Where I once loved to participate in meetings, I now dreaded sitting at the same table where I'd previously created supportive, smart and caring ways to enhance students' lives. The excitement became fear. The connection between team members became a time of disassociation. I began to behave as a puppy might, trying to please the person with the treat. I didn't know whether I should sit, retrieve or do them both to get the appreciation I so craved but also hated.

In my silence, I began to think about my abilities and my age. *What if I wasn't as good as I used to be? What if I couldn't connect with the students like I used to? What if others were looking at me like he was and wondering when I would be retiring? What if he was right and I no longer had much to offer?*

Then, by what seemed an accident, I peeked underneath the invisible cape I was wearing. And I saw myself again. My real self. The strong, spirited, gifted woman who likes to talk, who wears bright colors and scarves, and who has wonderful, time-tested wisdom that needs to be shared! I not only saw myself, *I found myself.* I took that cape off … and let that shit go. I quit the job I used to love. I walked out the door and didn't look back. In doing so, I found my voice. I became stronger in my purpose and I embraced my age. I embraced the wrinkles and the unexpected tinkles that make up this perfectly imperfect person that I am, right now, at the age I am. And I began living by the beautiful words of Vlada Mars: "We are connected by simple wishes: to be visible, to be heard, to know that we matter."

*About the author: Kim Kane is the award-winning author of "Sparkle On ... Women Aging in Gratitude" and a transitional life coach who helps women navigate through transitional times as they age. Her website and Facebook group provide valuable resources and offer a space for community and fun for women 50-plus. www.kimkaneandgratitude.com*

# a monarch emerges

By Jen Gilhoi

I remember loving myself. I was 8. I was very happy at home, where I could explore in the woods and meadow just down the hill beneath my bedroom window and read, write and draw to my heart's content. But that was not the whole of my existence. I would soon come to believe that the real world was made for bold, outspoken leaders and that I would always be a follower.

Despite this belief, I fought the notion internally—and often. I had what society might label as rebel tendencies and a desire to go against the status quo by questioning everything. Much later, I would come to connect these traits with an entrepreneurial spirit. Reflecting on those formative years, I see that I could have been embracing creativity. Rather, I began to loathe some of my behaviors and traits— mainly an intense shyness—that followed me everywhere.

My shyness compounded the drive for perfection. I'd do anything to avoid being seen. I started apologizing. A lot. *I'm sorry for this. Sorry for that.* I began to anticipate that I would not be enough. By my senior year of high school, after having the self-love beat out of me on a daily basis, I acquiesced and followed my peers on my first date with alcohol.

I quickly embraced that under the influence I felt

*un-self-loathe-able*. But as my relationship with alcohol progressed over two decades, this indestructible feeling, and this high, became more insatiable. It was met with equally matched self-loathing lows. I became quite the actress and high-functioning alcoholic, hopping on a spin bike the day after getting any amount of drunk, pedaling like mad to outrace my shame and frustration. *Why can't I control my drinking? What switch do I have that gets flipped and puts me in blackout? How did I embarrass myself last night?*

During these years, I retreated deeper and deeper into self-loathing and shame. I moved from questioning to knowing. *I am pathetic. I am not worthy of love. I am a bad person. I need to apologize.* This language of shame was brought about by myself, not by others calling out my actions and shaming me.

If I could talk to my younger self in active addiction, I would give her grace and support her like a beloved friend. I'd hold her truths. As Sonya Renee Taylor writes in "The Body Is Not an Apology: The Power of Radical Self-Love," "When we hear someone's truth and it strikes some deep part of our humanity, our own hidden shames, it can be easy to recoil in silence. We struggle to hold the truths of others because we have so rarely had the experience of having our own truths held."

In my experience, alcoholism is too big for many to hold. My truths were that I was (and still am, see Alcoholics Anonymous step one) powerless over alcohol. I had tried to help myself, but I couldn't. Others around me didn't know how to help, so collectively they smoothed things over and contributed to the normalizing and rationalizing of my behavior.

These were my truths before I walked into my first AA meeting. It was my first radical act of self-love in over two decades. I saw the community of souls seeking to triumph over addiction and desperately wanted them to hold my truths. And it was revealed to me that they could do so, empathetically, capably and comfortably.

I spoke my truth and they let it sit there in silence without fixing or advising. I listened to others' truths and understood that I was not alone in my most shameful behaviors. Exchanges in the rooms (as they're referred to in AA) carried me for over a year while I worked on step one: "We admitted we were powerless over alcohol—that our lives had become unmanageable." I fought, wrestled, relapsed and held breathless conversations with my higher power while running. Mercifully, one day at the end of a run the mantra "let go, let God" truly flowed through me. If I knew how to act unapologetically, I would have dropped to my knees. It was an absolute gift.

We remember those moments that have been gifted to us. Just last year, through a guided meditation practice, my imagination conjured up the meadow of my childhood. A gift awaited me there. It was a monarch butterfly, one of the millions that decorated the woods behind my childhood home during an annual stop along their migratory path. My butterfly flitted in during meditation, rich in color and vibrancy, striking in its dotted pattern, yet light and free. It instantly brought me back to the knowing, safeness and self-love I felt during my youth. It was different in this moment though. It was more powerful than self-acceptance, self-esteem or self-confidence, which I now know are external and fleeting. It was more grounded and innately true.

"We arrived on this planet as LOVE," Sonya reminds us. She notes that the early incidents in our lives are the yarn tethering our adult selves to our childhood histories of shame and isolation. My threads of yarn were shyness, sensitivity, the constant seeking of external validation, physical and emotional abuse, denial and perfectionism. And, of course, alcoholism.

My monarch reminds me that the ability to move from darkness to light lies within me. I am capable of holding my truths — even the uncomfortable ones — and allowing everything to exist while I remain in control of what I give energy and life to. If the world knows my truths labeled most shameful by society, I will not shatter. Stepping into hard truths with vulnerability proves that self-love is sustaining and it will always serve to evolve my story.

"Unapologetic action empowers us to make new stories, better than the ones we've been saddled with for years," writes Sonya. Ditch the stories, she emphatically encourages, "that have kept us from self-love. Humans made them up. You are humans. Make a better story."

*About the author: Jen Gilhoi is fascinated with the art of gathering and well-being. She began a sober lifestyle in 2014 and shares the story of her journey with the specific intention of smashing stigmas and as an invitation for others to engage in healthy self and societal inquiry. www.jengilhoi.com*

# a manuscript for reinvention

By Nazly De La Rosa

"You weren't supposed to be born, but something saved you and I can't imagine what my life would be like without you."

My mother told me the story of my birth and the days leading up to it when she had to make a decision whether to keep her pregnancy with me or terminate it. At the time, she was working as a secretary in a Catholic church in our native town of Barranquilla, Colombia. She was 24, married to my dad for seven years, and already a mom to my older brother, who was 7 years old and had been paralyzed at age 2 from a polio infection. In Colombia at that time, there were no elevators or parking spaces for the disabled. There was no special treatment for disabled children, and quality medical care was hard to come by. Through my mother's (and her family's) sheer determination, they managed to make life as normal as possible for my brother. But my mother was tired and all of her focus was on maintaining that life of normalcy for my brother. When she found out she was pregnant with me, she could not imagine how she would manage work, a disabled child, a baby and a tormented (but loving) husband. Her first instinct was to terminate the pregnancy.

She booked the appointment for that termination, and only her mother knew about it. What followed was a series of events that saved my life. Through what can only be described as divine intervention, the nuns and priests at the church where she worked found out about my mom's pregnancy. On the day I was supposed to be terminated, she walked into a surprise baby shower and baby basket full of clothes, bottles and handmade booties knitted by the nuns. As my mother describes it, she knew then and there that her child was sending her a message. I love to think of that moment when my soul—yet unborn—manifested an entire life. It would not be the first or second or 13th time I would do so.

At age 2, I waved goodbye to my father as he immigrated to the United States. At 5 years old, I hugged my brother and mother goodbye as they joined him after being granted a medical visa for my brother—one that did not include me. I stayed behind with my grandmother and aunt with the hope that it would only be a few weeks before I'd see them again. Weeks turned into months and months into years. During those years, I'd pretend to speak English. I would imagine what America was like. I would imagine what I would become after I arrived. I imagined, more than anything, being embraced by my mother's loving arms again. I created an entire world in my mind where I was already living in America.

In August of 1989, at 8 years old, my dreams finally came to life. A stranger accompanied me on a flight from Colombia to Newark International Airport in New Jersey. Within a month, I could speak, read and write perfect English. The learning curve was low because energetically I had already been that person for years.

I repeated this process of visualizing my transformation over and over for 39 years. Before I graduated high school, I already knew I would successfully get a bachelor's degree in journalism and mass communications. Before I finished college, I already knew I would one day look over the Manhattan skyline from my office. Before I met my partner, I already knew we'd have children. Before we had them, I already knew they would be boys. Before I left behind a lucrative marketing career, I already knew I would become a successful entrepreneur. Today, before disrupting the mental health industry and becoming a millionaire, I already know I will be one.

I have no psychic powers. I don't channel. I'm not a witch. I have simply tapped into a knowledge base that is available to everyone but that so few people take time to demystify in order to put it into practice. While it goes by many names—the law of attraction, manifestation, visualization, the Hermetic principles, and so on and so forth—the concept is the same: What you can imagine you can become. You create your tomorrow today.

My process is the same every time I wish to reinvent myself. There are mindset hacks that form my process, and they are the backbone of what is allowing my company, Believe It Life Coaching, to grow and to bring peace and growth to those who have not been able to find it—neither in church nor through their years in therapy.

This is my manuscript for reinvention: Focus on the feelings you want to have, not the things. Have a vision that not only allows you to become a better version of yourself, but that also benefits others. Do not allow yourself to be labeled—not by others, but more importantly not by yourself. You determine who you are always, and you can change that anytime. You will have to welcome change and cannot go where you're going as you are. You will have to be patient. The bigger the gap between where you are and where you're going, the more patience and trust will be required of you. You will have to see loss as beneficial. People who are not prepared to go with you where you're going will naturally fall off from your life. Failure and success are but varying degrees of the same energy. The universe is always conspiring in your favor. Enemies on a human level are friends on an energetic level. Improvements in yourself are never selfish. As you elevate yourself, you elevate the collective consciousness.

If you are here, you have a mission and an obligation to carry out your soul's plan. Everyone is significant. Your life has been a series of events leading you to the fulfillment of that mission.

*About the author: Nazly De La Rosa is "The Soul Coach," a certified life and spiritual coach and the owner of Believe It Life Coaching. Through her unique manuscript for reinvention, she is helping ambitious women to bridge the gap between the life they're living and the one they dream of living. www.believeitlifecoaching.com*

# just swinging

By Julie Sonnek

When I was 8 years old, with curly hair and a toothless grin, I raced off the bus to the smell of fresh baked monster cookies. All ooey and gooey, they were the perfect after-school snack. With a mouthful of oatmeal, peanut butter and M&M's, I'd relay to Mom, "I aced my spelling test" or "I held the flexed arm hang longer than any other girl in my class!" Running off to the grove, I'd hop on the tree swing next to Dad's machine shed. Peering up at the sun over freshly planted corn fields, I'd twist. Spinning and spinning and spinning. My firmly planted feet became barely touching tippy-toes. How many times could I twist without getting stuck? How dizzy could I get? Swinging was an experiment.

*Wood rots,*

*Rope frays,*

*Metal rusts,*

*Memories stay.*[1]

Growing up, home smelled of corn dust and manure. Home sounded like auger motors and combines, with directions bellered above the noise. From sunup to sundown, my parents toiled, bustled and bickered. Yet, amid the constant whirring sounds, home could be an empty place.

When I was 13, I slept over at my friend Kate's house nearly every weekend. Nothing was taboo at her place. Her mom gave all the good tips on makeup and tampons. Once I tried to tell my dad that I couldn't go to our family reunion, because I had made plans to go swimming with Kate and her family. He blew up and barked, "You're a Proehl, not a Landsteiner!" Running out to the play set Dad had built, I gripped the black braided rope and hoisted myself onto the sling swing. High into the air I disappeared, pumping angry and hard. Swinging was a release.

At 16, high school activities took center stage. I spent hours at school and didn't see the growing weight my father bore. My two older brothers had moved out some years before, and my grandfather continued to age. Without any brothers of his own, carrying the family farm became my father's burden alone.

One brisk December afternoon, shortly before my 17th birthday, my younger brother and I arrived home from school to see Mom standing outside. "Did you see the ambulance?" she asked.

"No, we took the gravel. Why? What happened?"

"Your dad swallowed some pills. He's been really down lately and sleeping a lot. Today I thought he'd been sleeping too long, so I looked in on him. I couldn't wake him."

For a moment, I stood frozen, until Mom asked, "Do you want

to come along to the hospital?"

"Yes, of course. Yes."

Later that night, knowing my father would live, I sought comfort under our old oak tree. Treading lightly over the crystallized earth, I grabbed hold of the ropes, stiff and cold between my gloved hands. Slouching up, I noticed how long and strong they were. Strong enough to dangle a body from the rafters. Thank God he went for the pills.

Low and slow. Back and forth. Tears streamed down my numbing cheeks. Swinging was a song of sorrow.

After high school, I left home for college, married during my senior year, and moved to Minneapolis for graduate school. By age 30, I was the mother of three. My days were filled with trips to the park swings for underdogs and chants of "Uno, dos, tres. ¡Más alto por favor!" Face to face, I held their small legs, guiding them to pump and push. Later, snuggled in for the night, we'd relive the day's play by reading Leslie Patricelli's bilingual board book, "Higher, Higher! ¡Más Alto! ¡Más Alto!" The pages were filled with a father pushing his little pigtailed girl over treetops and skyscrapers to outer space and beyond reality for an out-of-this-world experience. Swinging was exhilaration.

But like most perfect moments, these didn't last. As a young, often overwhelmed mother, depression frequently hijacked my happiness. I forgot how to listen to my body. I was afraid to allow myself to dance to the rhythm of my regrets or run to release the fury bottled inside of me. I couldn't remember to feed my sensory-seeking soul. Perhaps if I'd remembered how to spin, I might have been able to spiral right out of my self-destructive thoughts as quickly as they'd swirled in.

Sometimes I dreamed of another life. One night, after tucking my children in, I indulged in a traveler's click of curiosity. I discovered that people can swing at the edge of the world in Baños, Ecuador. High in the wilderness, a simple wood plank hangs from Casa del Arbol. Swinging became un sueño.

We held out on putting a swing in our suburban backyard until the COVID-19 pandemic hit. A swing set had always seemed superfluous living across the road from a city park. Quarantined at home, we decided to put up a pizza swing, flat and circular. My 10-year-old spends hours lying and swaying there, while my 9-year-old jumps and flips on our trampoline. My 13-year-old needs daily reminders to emerge from her dimly lit room, illuminated only by her screen's glow and a string of red LED lights. Some days, I fear she has already given up the magic in movement.

Nearing 40 now, I revisit the seasons of my life. During some, I desperately wanted to believe that a refreshing swing in the park could propel me over my anxiety and away from swelling feelings of hopelessness. But it couldn't. It can't. For a swing, no matter how high its arc, is stationary.

Much of the time, I am at peace being grounded right where I am. My work and play are here. I am doing the best I can to teach my children how to navigate their own seasons, the dark and the light. And if you happen to pass through my neighborhood and glance over to the park to catch a glimpse of the moon, you might find me there swinging, just swinging.

[1] *"The Swingset" by Grace Walton (Lines 1-4)*

*About the author: Julie Sonnek is a writer and K-12 language teacher. She writes creative non-fiction and poetry. Her writing has appeared in Literary Mama and Burningword Literary Journal. She has a self-published book of poetry and photography entitled "Una Vista Brillante: Reflections of Colombia," which is available at www.blurb.com.*

# the conversation

By Junita Flowers

I will never forget the conversation. Not because it was a beautiful exchange of grace or an impartation of wisdom. But because it was a truth-telling moment that painfully and dramatically transformed the trajectory of my life. The conversation was a wake-up call that reached far beyond my thoughts and gripped my soul. There I sat, wanting so desperately to be affirmed, valued and loved by another human to whom I had entrusted my heart. I wanted to be reassured that my life mattered.

The words hurt. The sound of every syllable rang inside my head and only grew louder as the vibration spread throughout my body searching for my heart, squeezing it like a sponge until it seemed there was nothing left. I was motionless as I processed the meaning of words I never wanted to hear but secretly wondered about.

I knew the relationship was toxic, but I didn't want it to be over. I knew I was emotionally empty, but somewhere along the way I learned to equate emptiness with selflessness and giving, so I wore it like a badge of honor. I was fully engaged in the fight to hold everything together, giving it all I had to keep from giving up. But this conversation was different. The words were different. They felt like an assault weapon delivering an immobilizing blow with the power of potentially being fatal. They broke me, but I couldn't afford to fall apart.

I wanted to be strong. I wanted to rationalize his insidious words as I searched for alternate truths. I wanted to be grateful for the gift of honesty and truth-telling, but it was laced with a poisonous venom meant for destroying hopes and killing dreams. My eyes began to swell and soon the tears rushed down my cheeks with a fierce and steady flow. My heart had been abandoned and my spirit was crushed. As I sat there feeling trapped in my own thoughts, I wondered if my heart had been abandoned because he didn't believe in me, or if it had been abandoned because for the first time I realized I had stopped believing in myself.

Reflecting upon this pivotal conversation that took place almost a decade ago still conjures up a myriad of emotions. So much loss happened during that exchange of words. The losses marked the beginning of a transformational growth process that led me on a path of purpose and self-discovery. Over time, I learned (and continue to learn) to embrace the change-making power of pain throughout the life cycle and its accompanying mandate to be acknowledged, felt and healed. Daily human existence seeks to celebrate strength and avoid pain. Conversely, life teaches us pain is inevitable—it's guaranteed. Its quest is to stir things up, while strength is an option that is measured solely through the weightiness of pain. *My life has been positively transformed through the presence of pain.*

I now understand the authoritative power of disruption armed with the uncertainty that's found in new beginnings. All those years ago, I had uncomfortably settled into a daily routine that masked my presence and silenced my voice. I set up residence in a comfortless zone where I nurtured the dreams of the outsider, while abandoning the heart of my very existence. I held on tightly to the walls of familiarity, offering a resemblance of shelter while void of safety. Dismantled by the winds of disruption and the chaos of discord, my comfortless zone had been demolished, propelling me full speed into the uncertainty and promise of a new beginning. *My life has been positively transformed through the presence of disruption.*

In the aftermath of that conversation of pseudo truth-telling and shaming, I have grown to appreciate the life-giving nourishment found in tears. Tears were a constant presence during those years. There were countless times when I cried so hard that my knees grew weak and I was on the verge of collapsing from the weight of sadness. The steady flow of tears became a source of cleansing and release, washing away the toxicity of hatred and abandonment, while incubating the seeds of self-love. *My life has been positively transformed through the life-giving nourishment found in tears.*

While time has allowed me to heal, I fully understand that inevitably life gets messy sometimes. But out of the messiness is the potential for transformation that's as beautiful as when the caterpillar ceases from crawling and begins to flutter in the wind with wings of a butterfly.

Indeed, I will never forget that conversation. Not because it was a beautiful exchange of grace or an impartation of wisdom, but because it was an awakening that resuscitated the hopes and dreams I had buried deep within. That conversation will forever be a part of my narrative, because from those words, I set out on a path of discovery where I found self-love and self-worth and learned to stand in my own truth.

*About the author: Junita Flowers is founder and CEO of Junita's Jar, a cookie company on a mission to share cookies, spark conversation and spread hope. In her TEDx talk, "It All Begins With Hope," Junita shares her journey of transformation. She's most proud to be mom to two amazing humans. www.junitasjar.com*

# breathe through it

By Anonymous

M y phone beeped. It was my sister, announcing via group text that she and her husband matched with an expectant mother. At this point, they had been waiting two years to pair with a woman who was willing to gift them her unborn child. My husband and I had been waiting over five.

"Congratulations! That's such fantastic news!" I texted back in silent heartbreak. I included a kitten sticker with a big YES across it. *That should suffice*, I thought. I awaited the onslaught of messages of joy to be showered upon them. I jumped in when appropriate. Then I left the group conversation as it naturally died down. I let out a big sigh and called my sister, who was ecstatic.

"Oh my God," she beamed. "I can't believe we matched!" She started telling me about when and where she found out the news. She said she cried.

"Of course you did," I shrugged, imagining the moment when my husband and I were to have such great news, the mere thought of the possibility filling my eyes with tears. But she kept beaming because she was elated. I kept asking questions because I wanted to be happy for her too.

*I am strong. I can do this. This is my most important role.*

*Swallow. Shut yourself down.*

A counselor I had been seeing about having kids said I should distance myself from friends who were in the process of becoming parents. "But that's not who I want to be," I had told her.

"You need to take care of yourself," she replied. I nodded because I knew she was right.

I wasn't able to give any joy without slowly ripping myself apart. Like a sturdy mama elephant tied to a wooden stake with a woven rope, I had developed what I grew to understand as *learned helplessness*—the surrendering of one's will to outside forces based on past failures. I believed I no longer had control of my journey to have a child. It was always going to be a sad, arduous path that was full of disappointment and dashed with other people's successes. The success was never going to be mine.

This all started in a hospital room. I was lying straight on my back with a catheter inside of me. My fists clenched. A nurse pressed her hand onto my shoulder. "Breathe through it," she calmly advised. "Deep breaths. Slowly."

I closed my eyes as the pain was constant. Blackness. Four little aqua dots appeared in my upper vision. I turned my head to look at the screen next to the table I was lying on. The screen revealed what the doctor was attempting to accomplish inside of me. Dye was supposed to fill me—first my cervix, then my uterus, then both of my fallopian tubes. He could not insert the dye into my fallopian tubes.

Instead, I watched it pool in a small area of my vagina near the opening of my cervix. The pressure this created forced me to turn my head and squint my eyes; they began tearing up.

"I don't want to hurt her more," the doctor said, withdrawing the long, thin metal straw from inside of me. I was aware that what was happening was not the desired result. The dye was not moving through my insides the way it was supposed to. I was having too much pain. Something was wrong. *I am infertile.*

I had somewhat already known this and told the doctor so. He looked at me intently. There were strong creases between his eyes, under the black eyeglasses I had complimented him on the day before. He was concerned. I told him it was OK. I was lighthearted at first, as the nurse helped me sit up. I was scared, but there was no more physical pain.

"I'm OK," I said again and walked myself to the changing room to reclothe in my own pants and T-shirt. I discarded the hospital gown into the laundry bin marked *soiled linen*. I drove home to tell my husband the news. Our conversation did not go well. The news tore our marriage and our lives.

But the news my sister was texting now was fantastic, and I wished so badly that sad tears were not my initial reaction. I wished I could share in her happiness appropriately. But I couldn't.

Four months later, just a few weeks from when her future son's birth mother was due, my sister learned by brutal and unfair means what tragedy the adoption process can extend. Her would-be birth mother had delivered a healthy baby boy a week prior and purposely did not inform my sister he had been born or that she would be keeping him. I received a quite different text that day: "Shittiest day ever. She's keeping the baby."

There had been a baby shower. A nursery had been built. There were loads of congratulations. And a tiny knit hat for the baby to wear home from the hospital, embroidered with the name my sister and her husband had chosen for him: Oliver.

I meekly called my sister on the phone to simply listen to her cry, because what else was there to do? Amazingly, a couple of weeks later, my sister had that answer: "You pull yourself up by your bootstraps and say, 'Okay. That sucked. What's next?'" Soon, she was sharing their adoption website on social media and connecting again with their adoption agency. She was determined to match with a new birth mother.

Here, I forgot to feel sorry for myself. "Is there anything I can do to help?" I asked.

"Get us out there. Help us match," she stated.

I went to my computer and began to write everyone I could think of who could help: *I am eagerly writing to you on behalf of my sister ...*

*Editors' note: This essay is published anonymously at the author's request.*

PUBLISH **HER**™

Publish Her is a female-founded indie publisher dedicated to supporting women authors.

www.publishherpress.com